Offerings at the Edge

Offerings at the Edge

Alexandra Kennedy

iUniverse, Inc.
New York Lincoln Shanghai

Offerings at the Edge

iUniverse books may be ordered through booksellers or by contacting:

iUniverse
2021 Pine Lake Road, Suite 100
Lincoln, NE 68512
www.iuniverse.com
1-800-Authors (1-800-288-4677)

ISBN-13: 978-0-595-43527-2 (pbk)
ISBN-13: 978-0-595-87853-6 (ebk)
ISBN-10: 0-595-43527-0 (pbk)
ISBN-10: 0-595-87853-9 (ebk)

Printed in the United States of America

For my mother,
Jane Taylor Banks,
With love

Contents

Introduction

The first poem of this collection found me on a Valentine's Day walk—somewhere between translucent blossoms and a river swollen with spring rains. More than forty poems followed over the next two years, inspired by such varied experiences as swimming with wild dolphins, buying shoes in a department store, gazing into the crater of an active volcano, and driving down Main Street. It's been both humbling and gratifying to be the steward of these poems. I never know when one will come, nor do I get to choose what I want to write about. For days before a poem emerges onto paper, I can feel it working deep in my body. As it begins to take form in an image, a phrase or occasionally as a whole poem, the excitement builds. The poem has to find its own flow, its own rhythm, its own message—and often turns out quite different from where I thought the first line might take it. It is thrilling to receive what Suzuki Roshi calls these "letters from the infinite".

These poems explore the way the world looks when I'm fully present, when I let life flow freely with all its unexpected rivers, when I open myself to everything as it is. It's then that the sacred shines through the most ordinary moments and this fleeting second meets an eternity of being.

Each moment is so precious—it has never manifested before just like this and it will never come again. Our challenge is to meet each moment fully, with all our senses, without judgment or concepts. When I wrote "The World is My Valentine", I did not know that this was the last walk I would take with my friend, who is now confined to his bed, unable to even walk across the room. It is comforting that, as his body shrinks, his spirit shines as brightly as it did that day when he sang with such jubilance into the freeway underpass.

This book is dedicated to my 93-year-old mother. More than anything else I have written, these poems seem to touch a place of knowing within her; she resonates with them in a way neither of us can explain. I am grateful that in her last years we have had the opportunity to connect in the rich territory of the soul.

I extend deep gratitude to my husband who is such a patient, challenging and wise editor, as well as the numerous friends and colleagues who have offered steady support, feedback, and humor: Robb and Sally Sals, Crystal Forthomme, George Levinson, Anina Van Alstine, to name just a few.

Finally, I offer this collection of poems up to the mystery that lives in us all and imbues this world with such stillness and joy.

Alexandra Kennedy

Initiations

What If

What if your body were just a suit of clothes
For a mystery—vast, open, empty?
An unknowable Presence that will be here still
When the glittering stars are extinguished.
A mystery quivering with the thrill
Of finding form in earthy flesh.
It waits to be discovered, not just here,
Hidden in this body—
But everywhere.

What if this mystery
Were looking through your eyes?
Not through the veil of thought
But seeing things just as they are—
The silent presence of this frail flower,
The sacredness of this smooth stone.
Exquisite beauty of mystery inhabiting form—
Each flower, each stone, each person
Your lost and found beloved.

What if this mystery
Were listening through your ears?
Listening to sounds just as they are—
They rise out of silence and return to it:
Sweet song of the meadowlark,
The hum of an airplane overhead,
The clock ticking.
The whole body alert and present,
Cells responding with a shiver of delight.

What if this mystery
Were expressing its love for itself
Through your eyes, your ears, your touch?
What if the clear space of infinite possibility
Knows itself through you?
Would you look at everything
As if it held a secret?

Shoes with a Secret

I never know when my next poem will come—
Driving down Main Street, feasting on fireworks,
Poised on a crater's edge, sipping water.
A small spark ignites in space,
Something shifts inside,
And words whirl,
At the threshold between silence and speech.

Today a poem paid me a visit in the shoe section
Of Gottshalks department store,
Amidst the clacking of cash registers and the hum of voices.
I held in my hand a slipper—
Soft, black,
Embroidered with flowers the color of cherries and apricots.

Suddenly I stop,
Step back into vastness.
Surprise blooms in the next breath.
Is that chorteling I hear from these rows of shoes?
Shoes with buckles, tassels, zippers,
Boots with fur peeking out the tops,
Black patent leather pumps with tiny silver beads,
Commonsense flats, flirtatious stilettos, robust running shoes.

All of them wink with glee, a hint of mischief.
Delighted in their startling secret:
Truth is hidden here too.
Inside these soles
Presence glows.
It throbs within everything.

Truth breaks the molds we try to create.
It won't be corralled
In temples, churches or teachers,
In prayer or meditation,
Or confined to the tips of mountains.

I'm grinning now—
Here in this department store
I could swear
These shoes are falling off their shelves—
Laughing.

Crazy Act of Courage

The moss green caterpillar undulates along a leaf,
A row of tiny round bellies slides up and down
As though driven by a thousand hungry mouths.
One day the caterpillar stops,
Ceases its voracious eating.
And in one act of courage or pure folly
Drops its plump body into blue space—
Tethered to a branch by a single thread,
Hangs upside down, exposed.

Then in a graceful sweep,
As though it has prepared for this all its life,
Turns its head upward,
And spins a sturdy cocoon around that green body.
Threads appear out of nowhere—
Sleight of hand,
Guided by a mystery,
Beyond anything we can ever understand.

In that dark womb, the caterpillar is no more,
Nor the butterfly that is to be.
In that instant, a chaotic soup of DNA,
Just possibility, no more form.

You, my friend of untamed tresses,
Sit in your green-walled room,
On your bed with posts entwined
With morning glories of cobalt blue,
Ivy spilling down—

A green kingdom for a caterpillar,
Before it was sealed in its tiny tomb.

You stop.
From deep inside comes an urgent prayer,
Filled with divine longing.
You want to be free of tortured thoughts.
You want to be at peace.

Are you at the point for your crazy act of courage?
Are you willing to be exposed and vulnerable?
Can you surrender to the currents of mystery stirring within you?
To accept that this life is no longer yours?
Are you ready to dissolve?
To travel back to your true source
To a place before the birth of galaxies,
Between thoughts,
To the stillness
At the center of your own being?

And most of all, can you become nothing?
To emerge from that womb when it is time—
But not before—
And spread your saffron wings
On currents that sweep you from flower to flower,
Sipping the luscious nectar of life,
Leaving trails of golden pollen everywhere you go.

Waking up

My friend is waking up
To the mystery she is.
Doesn't understand
Who lives in this body,
What stirs in her chest,
Why she smiles at nothing,
What sets her body humming.
She weeps seeing a single blossom of oxalis,
Petals of butter splashing sunshine in wild abandon.
She is turned inside out,
Nowhere to hide, no one to be.

She's had to abandon her ideas
Of God, of enlightenment,
Her seeking, her self-loathing, her self-knowing,
Even thinking that she is afraid.
There is no getting ready for this birth,
Only running toward her life, taking it all in her arms.
Everything she ever looked for is right here,
In this moment.

The mystery is waking up to itself,
In my friend with eyes of silver-blue.
The shimmering silence of the world waits patiently
To be reclaimed through these eyes,
Seen by the silent emptiness inside her.

You have to go back to being nothing,
Before you can become everything.

How Did I Miss All This Before?

I have stepped into this garden a hundred times.
Now each morning it is all new,
An invitation to wonder
Stillness breathes through everything.
Leaves glitter, wet with light.
The whir of wings,
A quivering flash of red-gold,
As a hummingbird deliberates
Over unopened tips of lavender,
Swelling with the promise of fragrance.

My body opens with this sweet, subtle stillness,
And I breathe in awe.
How did I miss all this before?
All those years I was busy searching
And missed what was right here, now.

Her hands flutter to her face—
Delicate hummingbirds,
Dabbing at persistent tears,
Tears that offer up the promise of sweetness
If she would just let them flow.
She has lost both her parents.
How fragile she feels—
Alone and empty.

Wake up! I want to say.
You are walking asleep.
If you can weep now for all that you have lost,
The grief will one day open a window

For the mystery to look out.
The world is waiting
To dazzle you with its beauty,
Waiting to welcome you home.

Grief is wise, I tell her,
It knows what you need to heal.
Trust this: surrender to the tides of grief.

In the oak tree outside,
A finch unleashes
A song so clear and tender
That it ravishes her heavy heart,
And tears begin to flow.
She weeps for her unlived life,
All the lost moments.

She rests now,
Released from the weight of memory,
Claimed by a new silence,
Her countenance luminous with a tender knowing
That some eternal mystery in her heart
Has come alive again.
She is here now, fully present,
To me sitting across from her, to the song of the finch.
In this moment, no longer asleep.
She asks,
How did I miss all this before?

Driving on Main Street

Driving my car, I glide through space,
The space out of which everything arises.
Main Street unfolds around me.
A woman bikes past, white skirt billowing,
Ruby leaves peek through foliage,
Shy harbingers of fall,
A feisty jay struts along a telephone wire,
Children wave from their lemonade stand
At the side of the road.

In wonder I gaze about,
Reveling in everything as it is—
Fresh, clear and shining.
Little sparks of delight beaming
From the heart of all things:
The cycling woman, the maple tree,
The iridescent jay, the plastic cups of lemonade.

Driving down this road, I have already arrived.
There is no distance to travel.
An alive, silent mystery pervades everything,
In the simplest things of this neighborhood.
This truth, so easy to dismiss—
Quiet, subtle, simple as a child at play—
Does not try to catch our attention.
Here it is in this moment, on this late summer day,
The same truth everywhere in miniscule miracles.
There is nowhere else to go to find it.

Just a few years ago I would have missed all this.
Consumed with thought,
I would have hurried along this familiar street,
Driven to an ever elusive destination,
Fueled by a hunger for something I couldn't grasp.
As if one more meditation, one more spiritual practice
Would assuage this terrible longing.

I did not realize that what I was seeking
Was on this very street,
In this very moment,
That what I was seeking
Was looking out these eyes
(hidden in the most obvious place),
That there was nothing more to search for.

The world is waiting to be remembered
Waiting patiently for eyes that can see.

Lois Rob

Fire Offerings

Sunrise

Above the sleepy blue canyon,
I wait for sunrise,
My feet planted on a sandstone ledge.

In a great bursting forth,
The first light flows over a smoky ridge,
Like a hundred blazing suns.

Everything tips into the light—
Twisted pines, soaring ravens, rocks glowing like flames,
All part of a mounting celebration.

We are this growing light,
We are this outpouring,
This torrent of joy that cannot be contained.

I let it all go, open my hands,
And fall
Into the sweet innocence of a child.

Everywhere I look this morning
There is a birth.
I revel in this new life.

Fire

I awoke this morning
To the sound of steady crackling.
First listening with eyes closed—
The popping and snapping growing louder.
Then looking out the window—
A conflagration in the empty field,
Red wings beating the air
In a frenzied dance of dissolution.

Later that day I cut dried branches
Of acacia and pine,
Heap pine needles on top
And light the pile in two places.
The tender flame starts slowly,
Tentatively tingeing edges of crumpled paper,
Then quickly spreads.
Roaring with delight,
Puffing up with gusts of wind,
It swallows all that is offered
And all that is hidden—
Its task to devour,
Without negotiation, without compromise.

Several years ago I dreamed that a fire
Had gutted my house—
Inside nothing left,
No studs, no walls, no floor,
Just charred space—
While the outside still stood like an ordinary house,
Looking as if someone lived there.

Fireworks

The night is our womb,
As we sit cocooned in blankets on the roof,
A circle of friends,
Faces upturned like small moons.
In the black dome overhead
Just a few stars burn clear.
Mars glows red near the horizon.
Emptiness becomes our canvas—
We are this space in which the universe unfolds.

We wait in the darkness.
A fireball shatters the silence,
Tiny seeds of stars—red, gold, silver, blue—
Erupt into existence,
Emanate in all directions.
With each shimmering shower of light
Our cells quiver with rapture,
As though something in us remembers
The Big Bang, the out rush of galaxies,
The thrust of life out of nothingness.
Even now those first stars swirl in our veins.

Something is burning at the center of my chest—
A small point of fire that blazes with the stuff of creation.
I sit with this growing pressure,
Restless, not knowing,
Waiting in the dark
For those shiny seeds of possibility
To burst into the spaces of my life—
A new beginning or discovery,

An insight, a poem or a song.
Within each one of us the Big Bang keeps unfolding—
New worlds, new galaxies explode through us,
Trailing infinity.

Offerings at the Edge

Here we are at the rim of Halema'uma'u Crater,
Seven women staring into this gray abyss,
Gasping at its strangeness, other-worldness.
Our gaze stretches into this vastness,
An utter void, slow silence unfolding into infinity.

Nowhere to hide here, all is exposed,
No distinctions, just emptiness.
Nothing familiar, nothing personal, nothing comforting
For the mind to hold on to—
Nothing but nothingness.
Our little separate selves shudder at the edge of this immensity—
How insignificant we are.

One by one we place our offerings at the rim—
Supple ti leaves, orange papayas, an owl feather.
Each one of us bends over our offering,
In silent prayer.

In a stroke of grace,
A young Hawaiian chants to Pele,
Ancient words of power
That rise out of the silence and swirl on the wind.
Words that call on her,
Fiery and fierce goddess of this volcano.

Are we ready to offer it all up,
All that we know—
To plunge into this void?
Are we ready to step off this precipice

Into the unknown?
To descend here feels like dying.

Our gaze goes deeper.
Whorls of steam rise from the floor of the crater
And a glowing mound of embers takes form,
Hinting at the power just under this gray crust—
Hot fire of creativity,
The fire of truth at the center of each of us,
Of all things.

Can Pele's fire take hold in our hearts,
Drive this burning into every moment, every act,
Expose all that is untrue in us—
The hurts, shame, unworthiness?
Can this burning jolt us back
To the truth of who we are—
The timeless infinity of this crater,
This deep silence, this nothingness?

Alexandra Kenr

Air Offerings

How Can You Dance with Emptiness?

In the middle of the night,
The house rests in dark stillness,
With a soft glow of moon,
My husband's lilting snores the only sound.

I am awake.
Humming cells conspire
To lure legs from under covers,
To slide feet along the floor,
Pulled to the open window.
The steady gaze of the moon and the flickering stars
Are cradled in an immensity of black space
That goes on and on into the night,
The same empty space within this body.

This body now begins to dance—
Arms sweep upward, slice through air,
Palms sculpt space.
Knees bend deep into the earth,
Gather roots.
As one hand scoops the rising sun,
The other draws down the moon.
Fingers flutter as sun and moon come together
In empty palms.

Each breath opens into mystery,
Births new shapes,
Unlocks blessings.
Surprised laughter as flowers open, babies blink,

And supernovas burst into being—
It is all here now.

The torso turns,
Feet step into a field of glistening moonlight,
As hands cascade down this chest,
Like clear mountain water finding its way to the sea.
Then another step,
One foot suspends in space,
And arms arch like wings,
Reach into emptiness.

All in perfect balance:
Movement and stillness,
Ascent and descent,
Inhale and exhale,
Lifting and falling.
Each movement arises out of emptiness
And returns to it.

No thought, no concept, no 'me',
Just wild wonder.
Joy moves from hand to chest to foot
In a river of bliss.

When this wide emptiness invites you to dance,
Will you try to fill such immensity with what you know,
Or let the true source of Being pour through you
In the great dance of life?

Ah, This Is Meditation!

I sit on a black cushion,
Facing an open window.
Trills of birds circle my head,
Silky whisper of wind brushes my cheek.
From behind a rustle of cloth,
A cough explodes in space.
Thoughts rise to the surface—
They dart about
Looking for food,
Then disappear into the dark depths.
All this, as it is, arising out of stillness.

I used to come to meditation
Like a warrior,
Ready to defend myself against the world—
Armed with earplugs, eye mask, blanket,
The window closed.
No sounds, no thoughts, no images to distract me
From the quest for truth within.

Now the window is wide open
There is nothing to defend—
No inside, no outside, no one sitting here.
In awe I rest in stillness
As life itself flows through.
Ah, this is meditation!

Clouds

The rains have passed.
Three clouds loll in a clear blue sky,
Billowy mounds of white froth—
Astonished to be floating in this immensity,
Giddy with the joy of being clouds,
Their very own expression of the mystery,
Exquisite forms arising out of infinite space.

On this crisp fall day,
With liquid amber trees flushing crimson,
I too am astonished that this mystery
Molds and animates my tender human form—
Pale freckled skin,
Wiry gold hair streaked with gray,
Eyes of verdigris.
How could I judge this body—
Want it stronger, firmer, younger—
When unimaginable power fires these cells,
When the rhythm of eternity
Flows through these veins?
How could I want to be anyone else
When there is only one of me in all of time?

Truth is as effortless as these giddy clouds
Being simply themselves.
I laugh out loud—
Teachers are everywhere.

Umbrella

Out the window,
Slivers of rain fall in silvery curtains,
Dissolving the world in gray mist.
An umbrella, the color of marigolds,
Slips by like a brief solar smile.
I laugh at the audacity of this small sun
Refusing to be extinguished by brooding clouds,
A bright yes to life.

Hurricane Ivan

From your spawning ground off the coast of Africa,
Primal nursery of civilization,
You spin across the Atlantic,
A white whirling spiral,
Long arms unfurling,
Gathering dark clouds, howling winds,
White tumbling water.
A moist galaxy,
You seek to grow, crave open space.

In the warm seas you expand your power,
Rouse sleeping waters, lash out in all directions.
You slap waves against land,
Whip trees, rip roofs.

At the heart of this wild frenzy,
A tranquil point of sudden stillness,
A point that contains all,
Transparent sky
Where all is sparkling and stars burn clear.
You circle this center like a whirling dervish,
For this is the secret of your power,
Silence at the heart of all things,
Emptiness that spins the worlds.

Your power humbles us,
Energizes our cells, cleanses the land.
Your ravage strips us of habit.
You open the floodgates to a vaster life,
Calling us back to the mystery.
Such wild love.

Full Moon

At the open window my cat and I
Gaze into the night.
The full moon paints the garden in a milky glow,
Brushing dabs of light on the tips of branches
And broad sweeping strokes across the roof.
Just two stars bear witness to this lunar presence
In the deep night,
A darkness now usurped
That can only hide in indigo shadows
At the foot of the maytens tree.

The constant chorus of crickets
Massages this bright world with sound,
A sound that springs joyfully from a deeper silence.
Inside houses people are riding the currents of sleep.
Their busy minds now turned to dreams and rest,
The world is restored to its natural stillness;
My cat and I breathe in this white night.

Lois Robin

Earth Offerings

Spring

Spring catches us by surprise,
Slipping between storms with a subtle smile.
She exhales sweetness into the air,
Stirs birds into a frenzy of song and flight,
Casts new colors into a wintry world—
Crocus yellows, raspberry pinks, bright greens.

She exhorts us to open our senses wide,
To throw open our arms to this explosion of life.
She will pull out the stops,
In her eagerness to waken this world out of sleep.

Spring ruffles edges of transparent blossoms
With her breath,
And warms us with a golden cascade of light.
In this wild contagion I don't know
Where my body ends or begins.

Fall

Nature saves her boldest colors for fall—
Leaves of copper, terracotta, crimson,
Sunsets that flare up with the brazen reds of dying stars—
As though to applaud this subtle threshold
When life pulls inward,
Releases what has come before.
A time when darkness grows.

In my yard the Chinese elm
Unfastens her green summer gown,
Without a sliver of regret.
Her coppery leaves tumble and float to the earth,
Without a whisper of resistance.
How proudly she exposes her skeleton of silvery limbs,
Without a trace of shame.

In autumn a layer of illusion peels back,
And stillness peeks through,
In crisp clear air, piles of crinkled leaves
And bare branches.
Spring and summer overflow
With sweet scents and ripe fruits,
But in fall we are called upon
To participate in this emptying of the world.

Winter

One white narcissus
Stands in a field of stillness—
This is winter's gift.

Dancing Barefoot

We kick off our sandals,
Hold hands, twirl and laugh.
Red-faced hibiscus,
Chattering minas perched on corners of roofs
Watch in wonder.
We dance barefoot in celebration
Of this morning,
Of the dropping of veils,
Of the moving through fear.

We are not confined to these bodies,
These separate selves.
The endless expanse of sparkling sky,
The flutter of wings,
And the soft grass under our feet
All move through us.

There is just this moment to live fully,
Without holding back.
Love flows out to everything we touch.
Blessings float down,
Petal by petal.

The World Is My Valentine

The world is my Valentine today.
Translucent blossoms, burst with exuberance,
As they exhale their fragrance into the air.
Bright green blades of grass
Press through cracks in the cement,
Growing as wholeheartedly as their kin,
Who just a few feet away,
Flourish in mounds of moist soil.

A woman with large dark eyes,
Her head wrapped in colored cloth,
Pushing a stroller across a footbridge,
Smiling as I smile,
A window that opens heart to heart.

The love pulling me like the river below
That sweeps spring rains down to the sea,
Foam sweetly surrendering
To the flow of rushing water.

My friend, beret perched on his head,
Laughing as he sings into the echoes of the freeway underpass,
Drawing surprised looks from drivers passing by.
The empty field where we stop
And breathe in the silence,
The hum of traffic at our backs.

So many sweethearts!
The beloved is everywhere,
Shouting, entreating, inviting
(If we would just be present long enough to hear):
Wake up!

I am inside you, closer than close,
Looking through your eyes!
And here, beaming from that blade of grass!
Here in the eyes of that woman!
Here in your friend!
And here in this field!
Celebrate this life, this earth, this mystery!
Wake up!
Remember that you are all this.

You are God's Valentine!

Spider's Web

This morning's surprise hides in the shiny air between two trees:
A perfect circle traced with two bands of crystal beads,
Still shimmering from last night's showers.
It hovers here,
Suspended by veins of lightning,
Like a window opening into space,
Framing transparent sky.

At the circle's outer edge its creator
Nudges from her mouth a slender thread,
Bright as quicksilver,
Tasting of eternity.
This web is her body—
A vibrating expanse
That she creates out of herself each day.
With every point connected,
She responds to each whisper of wind,
Each sudden jolt,
The slightest fluctuation.
This is her secret.

I bow to the truth in this moment,
To this spider,
So intent on her weaving,
Ever alert to a change of rhythm,
A shift of pressure.
As she spins silver-gray cords out of empty space,
I too create my world from within
Through threads of thought.
My life also unfolds in a vibrating web—
Vast and invisible—

Where nothing is separate,
All things connected.
And more registers in my body than I will ever understand.
So many connections that I barely grasp—
In a passing glance, seeming coincidences,
Stunning epiphanies.

All earths, all galaxies meet here in this point of space—
In a jeweled web

Bee Hive

What draws my gaze to this small hole
In redwood siding at the back of our house?
A drain outlet from our kitchen sink—
So ordinary, simple, unassuming.
The mind wants to move on,
But something else from within
Wants to fully experience what's here.
My body draws closer.

A soft humming fills my ears,
Hum of tiny wings beating the air,
As bees gather in a golden ring,
Dancing over one another as they pass inside.
What mystery is unfolding behind this wall,
What hidden work?

The beekeeper arrives in netted helmet.
With bare hands he gently pulls the floorboard away.
We are cast into a secret world—
A spiraling galaxy of thousands of bees,
A hive humming with music that spins the worlds,
Coils of gold mosaic dripping with amber honey,
Each bee consumed with a purpose,
Joyful to be part of a greater plan,
This flow of creation
That transforms flaxen pollen into sweet honey,
Honey fragrant with warm fields and laughing flowers.

The mystery at work in this hive is the same
That births star-studded nebula out of empty space,
The same mystery that flows through us—

In the most ordinary act,
When unimpeded by thought.

If the mystery has its way (which it always does in the end),
This hive's alchemy would take place in the chambers of our hearts.
Hidden work behind the wall of personality
Would transform grief into warm gold,
The soul just waiting
To pour itself into each new empty honeycomb.

Afternoon Walk on Prescott Road

The wind greets me first,
With whispers in the listening forest.
Then the voices of the stream,
The creaking of growing trees,
The raucous call of the jay—
Sounds that dance tender shoots
From the silent ground.

This valley gathers me in its green embrace.
Sunshine flows down in veins of light,
Through pungent limbs of pine, redwood and bay.
Lungs fill with the sweet exhale of trees,
Legs stretch out, eager to meet the earth
With each step.
This road leads nowhere but back to myself—
There is nothing here outside me.
Here I am—
In shiny blackberry nuggets, stalwart redwood trunks,
Miner's lettuce rinsed with light.

In the midst of all the changes
That make up this human life—
I am this source, this silence.
I am these roots of love.

Roots

The poplar tree that once reached lacy fingers to the sky
Is now a bleached wooden platform,
A stage for empty space to dance on.

Clumps of daisies look on, flaunting their yellow skirts,
As the fire of summer
Spawns multitudes of hungry shoots.
They press up through the earth along our driveway,
Lifting the asphalt floor onto their persistent shoulders.
Each shoot eager to burst into sunlit air,
Powered by its leafy dream.

The tree man tells me it's not enough to cut the poplar down.
Each root has its own life.
We must find each sprout
And pluck it from the ground—
If we're not to be overpowered by this insistent growth.

Isn't this the path of awakening?
I dance with empty space—
Space for freedom to flourish and life to flow freely,
Space for truth to emerge from this fertile void.

And yet I must be vigilant
To what emerges from the ground under my feet—
An absurd fear, a flash of envy, a small grudge.
Fragile filaments that look like nothing—
A thousand times we've faced them.

No matter how much we've emptied out,
Exposed the falsehoods of mind and heart,
There are still these tenacious shoots,
Ready to grow into full-fledged stories
Which we end up believing.

Harbinger of Dawn

It is past midnight,
My bedroom dissolved in ink-black darkness.
I am stirred from slumber
By a bird who cannot hold back her burst of song,
Eager to celebrate the dawn
That has not yet come.

Chirpings break out from startled kin,
Shaken from sleep.
But it is dark, not dawn,
And the notes dissolve on drowsy currents.
Silence again.

Hours later the sun blazes open,
Sending out its first yellow ripples.
The birds start up again,
An outpouring of song—
For the new day, for the fading night.
So much to celebrate
Each day a new discovery.

Lying in bed I listen for the song of that lone bird,
The harbinger of dawn,
Who sang with such exuberance
From that place deep inside
That knows that even in the darkest time
The light will return.

What Is This Love?

What is this love
That pours through me like a river,
Molten firewater that burns in my belly
And sets my cells spinning like tiny galaxies?

This love erupts for no reason—
In loud laughter,
In middle-of-the-night dances,
In unexpected kisses.

There is a vast empty field inside,
Soil dense, dark and fertile.
Every day something flowers there,
Rising from that silent ground,
Molded from this love.

Life spills out in all directions.
A stream of joy
That even the sky cannot contain.
Nor my heart that in this moment
Can only say
"Yes! The one I love is everywhere,"
And swoon with gratitude.

Alexandra Kennedy

Water Offerings

A Sip of Water

In my courtyard,
Slender liquid streams tumble
Through lions' mouths
Into a broad terracotta bowl,
Each drop celebrating its return with splashes and gurgles.
How water rejoices in this endless flowing,
With these clear sweet sounds.

I lift a glass of water,
Transparent substance perfectly molded
To this curved shape.
In my hand a miracle
That does not care to boast its life-giving power.
One sip and this clear liquid
Slides into my mouth,
Slips inside my body,
Releasing rapture to thirsty cells.
This same water that rose as mist,
Amassed as clouds,
And flowed down again as rain.
This water now flows through me,
Imprinted with silvery raindrops,
Wet earth and ocean swells.

I see myself swimming suspended in a tropical bay—
Clear blue water as far as I can see,
On the surface a powdering of sunshine;
Beneath a trackless void in which anything can appear.
I am free to move, undulate, dive.
No walls to come against.
No gravity to give me weight.

Nothing to take, to seize;
Everything to surrender, release—
Water slipping through my hands with each stroke.
Why hold back anything?

I am bathed in fluid infinity.
Warm seawater presses against my skin,
As though it wants to seep through
And dissolve the bubble of this body
Into the primal sea,
Return this little fragment of being
To the indivisible whole.
What ecstasy!

Water, you know how to flow, dissolve,
Smooth the hardest rock, change shape and form.
You rejoice as a single drop,
And celebrate your return to unbounded seas.

Teach me,
To welcome the currents of the unexpected,
To embrace the flow of inevitable change,
And to remember that a sip of water,
Seemingly so ordinary,
Is more sacred than I will ever know.

Dolphin Encounter

For years I watched you from the shore—
Gray-blue curves arching into the sea,
Glimpse of fin, flip of tail,
Enough to set me jumping on the sand,
Flinging my arms toward you.
I yearned to meet you
In your watery world.

This afternoon I slide
Into the clear waters of a tropical bay.
Slick black wet suit, bright blue fins and mask,
I look otherworldly.
I swim through aquamarine,
And float in outer space.

And you come,
Gliding in silence—
Sleek supple bodies, silver skin flashing,
Seeking, diving, turning, flowing,
Rising gracefully to where I hang suspended,
Astonished.

You are all around me now,
All these joyful bodies move as one being,
Undulating on light waves,
Splitting the surface of the sea,
Hurling through sky—
Triple spins that defy gravity.

You gather beneath, before, behind me,
With sweet secret smiles,
Eyes that open to clear being,

Presence with no judgment.
You welcome me,
Invite trust, laughter, play.

"Come swim with us," you seem to say,
"Sink into this ocean of Being.
Don't hover there on the surface.
Dive into this mystery. Dive!
Can you dare to be this joyful? This happy?"

One of you releases a luminescent bubble,
The size of a Christmas ornament,
Perfectly timed to float up to me—
A gift that I cup in my hands
And cry out with surprise and awe.

I match your pace,
And we meditate together.
Your wisdom melts into me.
In your presence I am no longer human.
I am spirit flowing out of body.
I am silence, stillness.

Hours pass.
And then as suddenly as you came you vanish,
Leaving a sea of blissful emptiness,
And laughter—
I can't stop laughing.

Turtle

On land I move with the quickness of a hummingbird.
In this gray-blue water, the texture of silk,
I move more slowly.
Flapping my fins I slip into the sleepy depths of this bay,
And glide over mounds of coral,
The oranges and yellows of Indian saris,
Woven with ribbons of glittering silver fish.

From the deep trough of stillness below,
A turtle is rising.
Long leathery flippers undulate in slow sweeps,
A measured steady pace, full of dignity and grace,
Even as he carries his home on his back—
A sturdy shell
Looking like some old map of this island,
With lava fields divided artfully into thirteen plots,
By the sure hand of an expert draughtsman.

"Here I am," he seems to tell me,
As we float side by side.
"Slow down."
He looks into my eye with an ancient tranquil gaze,
A simple look that opens out on a great inner sea,
With tides that rise from the depths of time,
And harmonize
With the movement of the moon and stars.

Turtle and I are rocked in a watery cradle,
Just full Being, present and effortless, as our eyes meet
Below the transparent pane of the ocean's surface.

No need to keep up,
No need to hurry.
Breathing slows,
Muscles relax,
And my body throbs with this slow song
Of belonging to the family of things.

Fierce Compassion

Sedna, Inuit goddess, you have pulled me
Into your cold ocean depths.
Turquoise waters turn black
And there is no solid ground,
Only a sinking into stillness.
There is nothing to hold on to,
As knots of pain shiver loose,
And loss flows out of its hiding places.

You know loss;
You know betrayal.
You know these depths, this cold darkness.
You are not afraid of its vastness.
You are not afraid of your power.

First your father betrayed you,
Forcing you to marry against your will.
Your husband betrayed you,
A cruel raven beneath a human mask.
Your father rescued you—
But to save himself in a raging storm,
Threw you overboard
And cut off your frozen clinging fingers,
One by one.

Each severed finger fell into white tipped waves
To become lithe dolphins,
Majestic whales, slippery seals.
All these fragments released back to the whole,
Where they cavort in primal seas.
You sank to the ocean floor—

Now a goddess,
Fierce protector of the oceans
And all her creatures.

I comb the algae from your hair,
As fish dart in and out like bits of topaz and jade.
Even in this brief moment of calm,
I feel your power, your outrage and sorrow
At the desecration of your seas.
From the still center of your being,
You whip up hurricanes and tsunamis—
A fist of destruction that sends seas screaming,
Winds pounding,
Bringing humans to their knees.
There can be no argument with this deep reckoning.

I live in this ocean.
These storms undo everything in my life.
I have never felt so empty, so porous.
I am willing to be this darkness (without expectation, without hope),
To be scoured out and carried by life's currents
To whatever destiny awaits.

Perhaps then this primal Feminine force
Arising from our depths
Will move through me
As fierce compassion,
As it wants—and needs—
To move through each woman on this earth.

Black Lava

We've come to watch the sun set at Honaunau, Place of Refuge,
Where tranquillity thrives within high stonewalls,
Where the land is saturated with serenity—
In groves of palm trees, pools of still water,
White coral sand.
Hawaiians have come here since ancient times
To pray for forgiveness.

Before the sun's glowing orb sinks into silence,
Our faces are suffused with golden light.
At this threshold between the world,
Where neither day nor night lay claim,
Judgment is suspended and we, too, pray.

Our eyes scan a blushing sky:
Perhaps we look for grace
That will stream from heaven
In translucent shafts of light,
Cascading in tiers onto a rocky landscape.

But the healing of our hearts
Does not come from above.
What will heal us lies beneath.
We sit on slabs of black lava,
A frozen river of ropes and swirls,
Once molten red, now the black of a starless sky—
A fertile darkness
In which nothing yet grows.

What can the lava tell us of its journey
To this perch at ocean's edge?
Did molten rock seethe and churn,

Gathering itself for that fiery eruption
Through earth's thin crust?

Did it pour out,
Consuming land in a steady river of fire,
Spilling secrets of earth's depths
Is this not how the planet creates itself—
Again and again?

Now earth's inner darkness is exposed in fields of black lava,
Vulnerable to the steady caress of sun, wind and waves—
A massage that will break down this hardness,
And transmute this density into rich soil
That can germinate bright green ti plants,
Colorful hibiscus, slender palms.

Will we, like the earth, call forth from the recesses of our hearts
All the hidden pain, self-hatred and jealousies?
Lay them out on the black lava on which we sit
For the sun of truth to illuminate
Without judgment, without blame?

Will we look on all this like the Black Madonna
Who sees all human frailties
And cradles the dark in us with such tender mercy?
Is this not forgiveness?

In the moment of pure seeing comes a subtle shift.
We discover the sun that dwells inside the dark,
The heart of bliss inside the knot of pain.
Resistance melts and sweetness streams into the world.

Waves slip between the boulders,
Cascade over rocks,

Settle into pools of shimmering silver.
Peace breathes through stone,
Rises from the waters at our feet,
Flows out to us on the last light from the sun.

As lava, palms, sky and sea all merge into night,
We welcome this deepening darkness.

Massage in Tulum

I am stretched out naked
On a massage table
In a small screened room in the Yucatan—
Ancient land of Mayan temples that perch on limestone cliffs
And rise like skyscrapers out of dense jungles,
Under a blazing sun.

A gecko clicks in the thatched roof overhead,
As lemon oil wafts through air heaving with heat.
Daniel's hands strong and certain,
Fingers of light pressing, probing, pulling, stretching,
Seeking out all the dark corners where little battles are waged:
A contraction here, an unexpressed sorrow there,
A buried trauma here, an imperceptible fear there—
Wherever the ever-changing flow of life has been resisted.

What can stay hidden with these persistent hands,
Drenched in spirit, aflame with fire?
Over each small knot,
Daniel chants and blows,
Breaking the mold of habit,
Clearing the space for spirit to descend.

Now a soft flowing of warm gold, a "yes" everywhere,
Sweetness behind the pain,
As my body is restored to its own rhythm,
The rhythm at the heart of everything.
This body like a smooth open sea,
Nothing solid.

No outside or inside—
Like water entering water.

The fire is lit:
Cells are charged with another intensity,
As vibration builds,
And sweeps through quivering limbs in an all engulfing tide,
A flood of power.
That shakes the table.

Daniel hovers over me,
Like a bird gliding endlessly with sun-tipped wings,
Eyes aglow with a tender knowing of this infusion of spirit,
Hands cradling my head.

I sit up,
As my hands dance to invisible currents,
As strange words take form in my mouth,
Unknown language of the spirit.
I pour myself out into the world
Through word and gesture.
This body is fragile, eternal,
Fiercely alive.

It is for this that I live.

Community Offerings

Winking Magnolia

I walk the narrow stone streets of the Ile St Louis,
Ancient village at the center of Paris.
Small shops allure with golden pastries,
Bright fabrics, sensuous leather shoes.
I peek in the dusky window of the Hotel de Jeu de Paummes—
Where vases of yellow lilies bloom boldly in a sea of lapis blue,
A concierge seated in a halo of light.

Seventeen years ago I stayed here with you—
Your stride long, steps deliberate as we explored this city,
Your blond hair curled neatly in a French twist,
Trim body dressed in elegant black.
Lover of Paris, of culture, of travel,
Seeker of those special moments
That flourish on foreign soil.
Everything becomes fresh
When we leave the terrain of habit,
Our known world.

Now your restless wings are folded in,
Protecting a body more vulnerable with age.
Slowing down you've come upon a rich new world—
In your home.
Tenderness has flowered in you
And a deep appreciation for small things—
A white magnolia winking in your garden,
The broad winged pelican circling the lagoon.
Nothing to drive you now, just life to savor.
Hasn't this sweet simple moment been calling to you all your life?

The Temple

Nestled unexpectedly in a clearing
Under a vast blue embrace of sky,
The Tibetan temple shines like a small jewel among the redwoods.
Poinsettia reds and lapis blues swirl over fluted edges,
While open-mouthed gold dragons
Perch ferociously at each corner,
As though guarding a secret treasure within.

This place is precious to me.
For years I have come here weekly to meditate,
Drawn by some mystery that breathes within these walls.
The door open, the temple empty,
And a freshly painted Buddha to greet me:
A young Siddhartha frolicking in a silken pool,
Bronze arm confidently reaching for the next stroke,
A restless seeker wandering in sea green mountains,
A grim renunciate seated cross-legged,
Long hair matted, black ribs protruding.
Buddha's life circles the room in one continuous band,
Each scene rolling into the next,
Guided by a monk's luminous, inspired hand.

Three years of painting before that knowing smile arrived.
In the panel above the entrance,
Buddha sits in the midst of the din of life,
In the midst of all the changes and uncertainties,
Still, silent (such a clear look!),
As the world flows freely around him.

I have shared in this creation of Buddhas.
A pilgrim on a marvelous adventure,

I walk these violet valleys,
Traverse cobalt streams,
To discover truths hidden in this menacing demon,
That frisky monkey in the apple tree,
For everything here has meaning,
And even the tiny songbird
May hold the key to the entire mystery.

This morning I have brought my 93-year-old mother to this temple.
We leave our small selves beside our shoes at the door,
Shed whispers,
And arm-in-arm step softly into stillness.

To step inside is like falling
Into the space within our own hearts,
The space inside our breaths.
Something is smiling here,
Transparent as air,
Simple, true.
This is the treasure
Just beneath this dazzling beauty:
This deep silence.
My mother feels it,
Is transfixed by it.
"I can't get over the feeling of this place—
This silence,"
She murmurs in awe.

She sinks gratefully onto a small couch in a corner,
And closes those ever vigilant eyes,
For here it is not beauty that catches her attention,
But something calling from within.

I am overcome with the sweetness of this wordless intimacy,
The love I feel for this frail and fiery woman
Who is my mother—
This quiet miracle at the heart of all things,
This blue flow of silence
That will take her home.

Dream of My Mother

At the side of the road,
Eucalyptus leaves curl like crescent moons—
Their fullness long past,
All that supple silver-green turned to brittle brown
On their journey back to earth.

In a dream I push open my mother's bedroom door,
Her body curled crescent-like on the floor.
I kneel in violet shadows, take her in my arms—
The knotted fingers I know so well, eyes a glassy blue.
Ninety-three years of audacious living fall back into silence,
As I rock her torso to waves of prayer.

My bones tremble, with the knowing
That this death will change my life.
I breathe in aloneness,
All-one-ness.

We are all on our journey back to earth,
Back to silence.

When the Lead Duck Falls Away:
For My Stepfather

At dawn in sweet silence
You slipped out of your body—
Such a quiet, graceful exit.
You were never one to cause a commotion.

All day we've seen you passing,
Winging weightless,
In flocks of white-striped ducks—
Heading home again.
In snowy egrets
Fishing in the still water of the bay,
All elegance, exquisitely calm.

You've left us at the shores of silence,
Our hearts hanging somewhere in space,
Sad and disoriented,
As when the lead duck falls away.

You are precious to this earth,
And through the earth you remain with us—
In the swooping flight of terns,
In these snowy egrets,
In every act of kindness,
Inside each breath.

Shiny Truths Dancing Everywhere

My friend and I sit in a courtyard
At a small table with a black screen top,
Strong enough to hold our cups,
But more space than matter.
We sip green tea.

Pigeons flutter at our feet,
Soft sound of voices from other tables,
A feather floats down,
Snow-white as my friend's blouse.
I welcome its lightness, its message.
Everything is significant,
Not separate from the rest.

We have not spent time together for three years.
We have not truly met.
We speak of her painting, horse, and family.
We speak of her homeland in Wales.

I rest in silence, listening to her voice,
To the whir of wings and the click of cups.
I watch the smallest movement in me
To protect, to defend.
I do not want to hold back.
I want to meet her fully in the spirit of discovery.
I want the words to flow from a place of truth,
That what we say here is what needs to be said.

I share with her my world—
Inner shifts, my son, the death of my cat.
Birds rustle the leaves over our heads,

And a milky heap, the size of a coin.
Even the pigeons seem to be participating in our conversation.

I pause, pull back,
Settle into stillness.
Then the beginning of a clear flowing,
A sudden urging from the center of my being.
Everything loosens.

I bend closer, elbows on the table,
Leaning toward my friend.
We move into the territory of the heart.
The spark of connection ignited,
We go deeper.
I ask what was happening when she pulled away.
I speak of the uneasy feelings in my body,
Of the urge to speak and the holding back.
How the years slipped by,
Without connecting.

It is not easy to speak of these things,
But this is the dark fertile compost of relationship.
We turn over feelings that have been hidden,
Inviting the heat of truth to transform this confusion.
Even as I speak, I know all this is
Already healed, already past.
Without knowing why,
The shadows have dissolved.
Perhaps the simple fact of our being here.

A bird glides by,
Gray wings beating the space
That has opened up around us.
Breathing is easier,

Smiles flicker,
A clear-sighted softness settles in.
There is nothing more to say.

As we stand to leave, we hug.
And the whole courtyard pulses in my arms.
The pigeons, the rustling leaves, these human beings
Are all part of the rhythm of life flowing,
Shiny truths dancing everywhere.

The World Is Your Home

From Paris to Brussels we've come,
Brimming with the beauty and culture
That Paris generously grants her visitors,
Yet starved for kindness,
For a look without wall,
For hearts that break loose.
In the streets no one looked up, met our eyes.
Waiters scoffed at our questions.
So little laughter, so little warmth,
No sense of welcome.

At the revolving door of the Brussels hotel,
You step out to greet us, a beacon of being,
Your smile spreading toward us like a blessing,
Nose broad, skin the color of cocoa,
Your open palm seeking ours in welcome,
As large dark eyes glisten with the urge to live fully,
To connect.

As you carry our luggage,
Your laughter fills the lobby's open space,
Where glass elevators glide up and down
And fountains gurgle in black pools beneath.
We are washed by your warmth.

Jacob, you are far from your home
In the Cote d'Ivoire,
And yet your smile tells me
You know that the same mystery that lives in you lives in me.
We live in different bodies,
Different countries,

Different cultures,
But we are the same in essence.
There is no separation.

You have made the world your home,
And this ordinary meeting
Yet another moment to shine.

For My High School Friend Jenny

You flew across our threshold—
Chestnut wings unfurled, feet barely touching the ground.
Small boned, vital, fluttering,
You move with the charm of a birdsong.

We were teenagers together—
Dreaming about the lives we thought we wanted,
Fussing over the bodies we were growing into.
Now we've left our old voices behind.

We engage again.
It's no longer our history that we share.
But the silence that gives birth to our words,
We meet in the spaces of our conversation—
Heart to heart.

Our friendship is as fresh
As that wild, curling blade of grass
That just spiraled from the ground this morning.

Mezza

She slips silently into the garden—
Nibbles tender tips of catmint,
Nestles on a patch of earth,
Invites the sun to slide buttery fingers
Over her ruffled fur,
To caress and warm her frail body.

She drinks in big gulps of life,
Eyes the color of mottled sunflowers, half-closed,
Ears cocked toward the cricket clicking behind her,
The chatter of jays overhead.
Not one thought of dying on this spring day,
Even as her kidneys resign their task,
And a small pebble of tumor grows in her belly.

She is fully present
In this exquisite marriage of sun and song,
A teacher for me even now in her final days—
"Sit here with me", she says,
And I breathe it all in—
The sweetness and surrender wafting from her body,
The riotous spring,
And more love than my heart can hold.

Pure, Simple Being

You dropped into our hands like a spring blossom,
All sweetness, all heart.
No story of your past,
No secrets, everything contained here, now.
With your head resting in my lap,
Eyes glistening black like the space between stars,
My hands stroke fur powdered with warm gold.

For you there is no great work,
Only this moment to be met,
Fully and completely.
Eyes watch in wonder,
Ears alert to each whispering sound.
Joy spills out through a wagging tail
And tiny shivers of delight.
You greet each person
As though there is no life outside this meeting,
And love perfumes the air.

What is it that in your presence masks fall away,
People smile, glow,
Open up like flowers?
You offer pure simple being
And an ancient faithfulness.

We humans are evolving beings
With so much to learn about living from the heart,
About the power of simply being.
Teach us, Zoe, what you live so naturally, so effortlessly.
Teach us how to love.

Your Spacious Heart:
For Jon

I love the way your eyes open in the morning,
Azure sky peering out from under drowsy lids.
I love the way your long fingers caress a keyboard,
Coaxing music from your soul.
I love the way you speak your truth,
Without apology, with integrity.
I love the way you are aging, with humor, humility and grace.
I love your everyday acts of kindness.
I love the way you care for me, with hands wide open.
I love your spacious heart, your passion, your big dreams.

The same source that flows through your eyes, ears, lips and fingers
Flows through mine.
And yet what an exquisite unique expression
You carry into this world.
I am blessed by your presence and love.

Alexandra Ker

Closing Offerings

Sinking into Silence

Sinking into silence,
Silence of soft snow.
Deeper still,
Stillness of a clear night.
An essence that saturates every cell,
Gives birth to love, to stars,
To smiles that linger on lips.

A silence not separate from sound—
The swish of wheels on wet streets,
Wind whispering through trees,
Water splashing from a storm drain,
Waves hissing along the shore,
Carrying the thrill of the entire sea.
The sound of God laughing
In vast empty space.

Silence never leaves us.
Where could it go?
It's we who leave it.
Our noisy minds lead us
Away from our true home.

Sink into the silence that is here now—
Inside you,
In this moment,
In this sound,
This tree, these eyes.

Let this silence bring you home,
And the sweet smile of Buddhas
Spring to your lips.

That wind is your breath.
Those waves are your pulse.
This silence is who you are.

Stopping the Words

Eight women sitting on a lava wall,
Shoulder to shoulder,
Wrapped in silence,
Linked in simple being,
Faces aglow with the last splash of light.

The rocks at our feet slip into shadows,
As forms are softly swallowed by a thirsty twilight.
The ending of the day and yet the beginning,
Stopping the words,
The new world is already here.
We are born in this silence.

978-0-595-43527
0-595-43527-0

Made in the USA
Las Vegas, NV
11 February 2022

43703966R00069